W9-ARQ-332

Rosa Bonheur

Robyn Montana Turner

Little, Brown and Company
Boston   Toronto   London

To Trent — firstborn —
who loves animals and realistic art

ACKNOWLEDGMENTS
I'd like to extend my grateful appreciation to the many individuals who influenced
the development of this series and this book, including Maria Modugno and her
assistant editor, Hilary M. Breed, for tenaciously seeing this book through to
completion; Virginia A. Creeden for gathering permissions for the images from around
the world; Eric, Sarah, and Madame Louis Sorrel Dejerine of the Château de By; my
mother and daughter for reviewing the manuscript and providing insight; my father,
son, other family members, and friends for their encouragement; Dr. Renee Sandell;
other biographers of women artists; and the many museums and collectors whose
photographs appear in the series.

First Paperback Edition

Quotation on back jacket and page 3 excerpted from *Rosa Bonheur: A Life and a
Legend* by Dore Ashton and Denise Brown Hare. Copyright © 1981 by Dore Ashton
and Denise Brown Hare. Reprinted by permission of Viking Penguin, a division of
Penguin Books USA Inc.
As the captions indicate, the location of some of the artworks reproduced in this
book are unknown. Works credited to Anna Klumpke are reproductions obtained from
Ms. Klumpke's biography of Rosa Bonheur, *Rosa Bonheur: Sa Vie, Son Oeuvre.* Paris:
Flammarion, 1908.

Library of Congress Cataloging-in-Publication Data

Turner, Robyn.
    Rosa Bonheur : portraits of women artists for children / by Robyn Montana
Turner. — 1st ed.
        p.   cm.
    Summary: A biography of the French artist renowned for her sensitive, realistic
paintings of animals and her portrayals of the American West.
    ISBN 0-316-85648-7 (hc)
    ISBN 0-316-85653-3 (pb)
    1. Bonheur, Rosa, 1822–1899 — Juvenile literature.   2. Painters —
France — Biography — Juvenile literature.   [1. Bonheur, Rosa,
1822–1899.   2. Artists.]   I. Title.
    ND553.B6T87   1991
    759.4 — dc20
    [B]
    [92]   90-44135

10 9 8 7 6 5 4 3 2 1

TWP

Published simultaneously in Canada
by Little, Brown & Company (Canada) Limited

Printed in Singapore

The eye is the route of the soul, and the pencil or brush must sincerely and naïvely reproduce what it sees.

— Rosa Bonheur

Rosa Bonheur
(bon-ERR)
1822–1899

Just 150 years ago, only a few women in the world had become well known as artists. Since then many women have been recognized for their artwork. Today some very famous artists are women.

Nowadays both boys and girls are encouraged to become great artists by attending the best art schools, where they study together with the finest art teachers. Both men and women learn to draw, paint, and sculpt images of the human body by studying nude models.

But if you went back in time to France during the mid-1800s, you might wonder why women artists were not allowed to attend the best schools of art. You might be surprised to discover that women were not permitted to look at nude models to help them portray the human figure. And you probably would be disappointed to learn that most young girls were not encouraged to become great artists.

During that time, more than 150 years ago in France, there lived a woman who became well known as an artist anyway. Her name was Rosa Bonheur. Today her works of art hang in museums throughout the world.

Auguste Bonheur. **Portrait of Rosa Bonheur.** *1846. Oil. Bordeaux Musée des Beaux-Arts. Reproduction © Musée des Beaux-Arts de Bordeaux.* This portrait was painted by Rosa's younger brother when he was twenty-two. It was shown in the Salon of 1848, a Paris exhibition and contest in which Rosa's family entered six drawings and two sculptures.

Raymond Bonheur. **Portrait
of Rosa and Auguste
Bonheur.** *1827. Oil. Bordeaux
Musée des Beaux-Arts.
Reproduction © Musée des
Beaux-Arts de Bordeaux.*

On March 16, 1822, in Bordeaux, France, Sophie Marquis and Raymond Oscar-Marie Bonheur became the parents of a baby girl. The French couple named their firstborn child Marie Rosalie Bonheur. Later they would call her Rosa Bonheur.

The French name Bonheur, which means happiness, was just right for this cheerful baby. Prosperity and good fortune, two more meanings of Bonheur, would also apply to Rosa as an artist later in life.

When Rosa was two years old, her brother Auguste was born. The Bonheur family lived with Rosa's grandparents, who loved the children very much. Rosa's deep, dark eyes were filled with playful mischief. Her square chin and sharp nose made her appear determined even as a tiny, round child. The dark brown curls that surrounded Rosa's face shone in the sunlight. Who would have guessed that many years later a Rosa Bonheur doll looking like this healthy little girl would be created in honor of the famous artist?

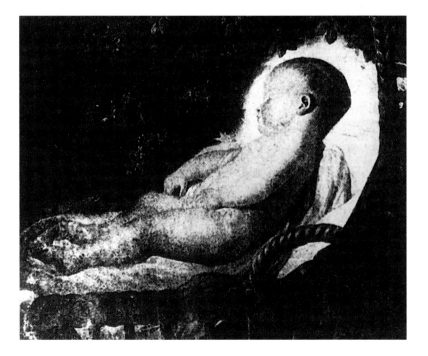

Raymond Bonheur. **The Infant Rosa Bonheur.** *1823. Oil. Anna Klumpke. Courtesy of Madame Louis Sorrel Dejerine.*
Raymond painted this portrait of Rosa, his firstborn child. Only a few of his paintings can be found today.

Sophie Bonheur loved to work and play with Rosa. She encouraged her very young daughter to draw, and she often sang to her at the piano. Sophie invented a way of teaching Rosa to read by asking her to write letters of the alphabet beside the little girl's drawings of animals. Next to a cow Rosa learned to write a C, and beside a bird she wrote a B. Since Rosa loved the animals that she drew, she grew to like the alphabet and words, too.

Raymond Bonheur. **Rosa at Four.** *1826. Oil. Studio Museum at the Château de By. Courtesy of Madame Louis Sorrel Dejerine.* Rosa learned to read by adding letters to the pictures she drew.

Rosa was allowed to run about freely. She liked to romp through the colorful gardens of friends' country estates. Since Rosa loved animals so much, her mother let her play in the horse stables near the gardens. Inside her house, Rosa was allowed to cover the white walls with her carefree sketches as high as she could reach. Next she learned to design and cut out paper animals. Soon her drawings of animals became her mother's favorite artworks.

Even though most of society did not encourage girls to become artists, Raymond hoped his daughter would grow up to create works of art as good as those of Elisabeth Vigée-Lebrun, one of the few well-known women artists of the time. As an artist, he looked forward to teaching Rosa about art, just as Elisabeth Vigée-Lebrun's father — also an artist — had taught his own daughter to paint.

Over the years, the Bonheur family continued to grow. By the time Rosa was five years old, she had two younger brothers, Auguste and Isidore. In order to support the family, both of Rosa's parents worked. Sophie earned a living by giving piano lessons, and Raymond taught drawing. Both parents loved their family very much, so it was no wonder that six-year-old Rosa became upset when her father moved alone to Paris. He wished to improve his artistic skills and study religion. In Sophie's letters to Raymond, she wrote that Rosa asked every day when he would come back. Rosa painted pictures of little men to send her father while he was away.

Raymond Oscar-Marie Bonheur. **Self-Portrait.** *1823. Oil. Anna Klumpke. Courtesy of Madame Louis Sorrel Dejerine.*

Raymond Bonheur. **Sophie Bonheur with Her Children Auguste and Rosa.** *1827. Anna Klumpke. Courtesy of Madame Louis Sorrel Dejerine.*

After a year of being apart, Sophie, the children, and their grandmother took a two-and-a-half day stagecoach trip from Bordeaux to Paris to live with Raymond. The next year, in 1830, Rosa's sister, Juliette, was born. Soon Raymond left the family again to join the Saint-Simonians, a religious group whose political beliefs included equal rights for women and men. When he returned three years later, Sophie became ill and died. She had worked too hard to take care of the family. By that time both of Rosa's grandparents had died, too, so Raymond was left with the four children.

At age eleven Rosa suddenly found her family life in a shambles. She was very sad. Raymond sent Juliette from their home in Paris to live for a while with a friend in Bordeaux. Rosa's brothers were sent to a nearby boarding school, where Raymond gave art lessons in order to pay their tuition. Both Rosa and her father hoped she could study art at school. But because Rosa was a girl, Raymond began to fear that she would not be able to earn a living as an artist and should study something more profitable.

In those times, a common trade for girls to learn was dressmaking, so Rosa was sent across town to live with Madame Gendorf to be trained as a dressmaker. Rosa didn't like dressmaking, and she often sneaked out of her lessons to turn the crank on the woodworking machines — lathes — in Monsieur Gendorf's woodcarving shop behind the school. Soon Rosa was sent home to her father.

Raymond tried a second time to place his daughter in a school. This time, in exchange for his drawing instruction at Madame Gilbert's boarding school, he arranged for Rosa to have a scholarship there. As was the custom in schools for the well-to-do, the girls brought their own eating utensils and other belongings. Rosa's knife, fork, and spoon were not made of silver. Her clothes were inexpensive, and she had no pocket money. Rosa's classmates made fun of her, which made her angry. Her temper flared easily. When she wasn't fussing with her friends, she taught them to play wild games during which they stomped all over the flower gardens. Once again, the rowdy girl was sent home.

Jean Baptiste Camille Corot (1796–1875). **Portrait of a Child.** *Oil on wood. 12⅝ × 9¼ inches. The Metropolitan Museum of Art, bequest of Mrs. H. O. Havemeyer, 1929. The H. O. Havemeyer Collection (29.100.564). Photograph by Malcolm Varon.* For more than 150 years, people have thought that the model for this portrait was Rosa Bonheur. However, Anna Klumpke, a friend during the last years of Rosa's life, believed the model was instead an unknown boy.

Rosa Bonheur. **Sketch of a horse's head.** *1835. Anna Klumpke. Photograph: Princeton University Libraries. Marquand Library.*

Raymond realized that traditional schools for girls did not suit his firstborn child. Finally he decided that Rosa could stay at home in his art studio. He let her work with a variety of media — drawing, painting, and sculpting. There, in her father's art studio, Rosa's education as an artist began.

All day long she practiced. Every morning her father gave Rosa a task. Sometimes she was to copy an engraving or a plaster cast or a still life of flowers and fruit. One day Raymond arrived home and found that instead of copying, Rosa was creating her very own painting of a bunch of cherries. He was so impressed that he formally took her on as one of his art students. Her first assignment was to begin a study of landscapes and animals. Finally Rosa had found a "school" that she loved.

The next year, when Rosa was fourteen, her father sent her each day to the Louvre (LOO-vr), the world-famous art museum in Paris. There she practiced her art skills by copying paintings by famous artists — mostly men — who had lived hundreds of years before her. Rosa stayed all day every day at the Louvre. She lunched on bread, a penny's worth of fried potatoes, and a mug of water taken from the fountain in the courtyard. Women and girls were allowed to study in this beautiful art museum, even though they were not permitted to study in the best schools of art. Rosa was the youngest girl-student at the Louvre, and sometimes the older students and visitors chuckled at her. But Rosa didn't care. She even sold a few of her paintings to them.

E. Baldus. **The Louvre** (view of the Napoléon courtyard during the Second Empire). *Reproduction from Musées Nationaux—Paris. © Photo R.M.N.*
When Rosa practiced painting at the Louvre, the famous museum looked like this. Today the Louvre contains even more world-famous works of art, and visitors enter through a large, modern room with a glass roof in the shape of a pyramid.

During that same year, in 1836, Raymond was asked to paint a portrait of Nathalie, the twelve-year-old daughter of the well-to-do Monsieur and Madame Micas. During this time Rosa and Nathalie developed a friendship that would last the rest of their lives. The Micases loved Rosa as a daughter, and they encouraged her to visit often with Nathalie, who was in poor health.

Soon Rosa's brothers, now young teenagers, returned home. During the next several years, the four children and their father formed a close family unit. Each evening they all drew and painted together. Still, Raymond was concerned about Rosa's lack of formal academic education, and he encouraged her to read about French history each night after the evening meal.

Rosa Bonheur. **Rabbits Nibbling Carrots.** *1840. Oil. Bordeaux Musée des Beaux-Arts. Reproduction © Musée des Beaux-Arts de Bordeaux.* Rosa entered this painting in the Salon of 1841. When the art critics said nothing about it, she accepted their silence with glee.

In 1841, when she was only nineteen, Rosa had her first exhibit at the Salon, an annual art show in Paris. By then she knew that animals were her favorite subject, and she entered her oil painting *Rabbits Nibbling Carrots.* Rosa had done a remarkable job in creating the soft texture of the rabbits' fur by painting hundreds of fine lines. She placed the light color values of the paints against the dark color values to create contrast. And she positioned the two rabbits somewhat evenly on her canvas to show symmetrical balance.

The art critics had nothing to say about the painting, which delighted Rosa and her father. After all, at that time — when women were not recognized as artists — no criticism from the art critics was a silent victory for Rosa.

In that same Salon of 1841, Rosa also entered her three-dimensional bronze artworks, or sculptures. The proportions of these animal forms were so realistic that they looked exactly like the actual rabbits, sheep, and goats. People loved to hold Rosa's sculptures. The small bronze forms were judged favorably by the art critics, and they became popular items for purchase as gifts and home decorations.

Rosa Bonheur. **Ewe Grazing.** *No date. Bronze. Courtesy of The R. W. Norton Art Gallery, Shreveport, Louisiana.* In addition to her painting and drawing, Rosa excelled at sculpting. Rosa chose not to become a sculptor, however, to avoid competition with her favorite brother, Isidore, who was also an excellent sculptor.

Later in that same year, the family moved to another apartment in Paris on the rue Rumford, or Rumford Street. The neighborhood was perfect for Rosa, as it was near fields and farms, where she could study the landscape and observe animals in the beauty of their natural surroundings. The Bonheurs now had a large studio on the sixth floor above their apartment. Inside the studio they kept ducks, rabbits, quail, birds, a goat, a squirrel, and a sheep. Each day young Isidore carried the sheep down six flights of stairs to the fields so that it could get some fresh air and exercise.

In 1842 the carefree Bonheur household suddenly acquired a sense of order. Rosa's father married Marguerite Peyrol, who had a time and a place for just about everything.

Rosa Bonheur. **Shepherd and His Sheep.** *1841. Oil. Anna Klumpke. Photograph: Princeton University Libraries. Marquand Library.* Rosa painted this pastoral scene during the time the Bonheur studio in Paris was filled with animals. Perhaps one of the sheep in this painting was carried by Isidore up and down the stairs. Might the shepherd be Isidore?

But Rosa, now a young woman of twenty years, paid little attention to her new surroundings. By this time she had become even more fascinated with art, and she began to study paintings of horses by famous artists such as Théodore Géricault and Eugène Delacroix. She observed the animals at horse fairs. She cut up animal parts from the butcher's market and made drawings of the muscles and bones. Using a variety of lines, shapes, and textures, she practiced drawing horses and other animals. Rosa's drawings and paintings improved.

Rosa Bonheur. **Birds in the Studio.** *1841. Drawing. Anna Klumpke. Photograph: Princeton University Libraries. Marquand Library.*

Rosa Bonheur. **Mallard Ducks.** *1846. Ink. Anna Klumpke. Photograph: Princeton University Libraries. Marquand Library.*

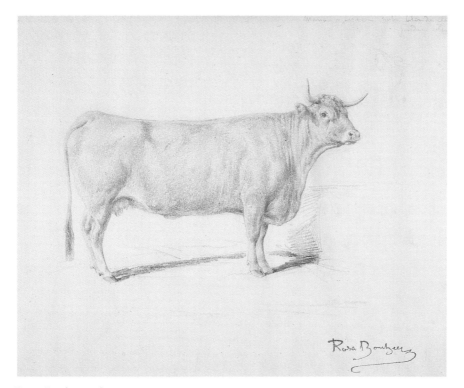

Still Rosa wasn't satisfied with her own works of art. She knew that Géricault and other artists had studied cattle in the slaughterhouses, where they were butchered. So in 1845 it seemed only natural to Rosa that she, too, should observe the livestock there, even though it would be painful to watch the suffering. The prize animals, surrounded by pools of blood, were often frightened and restless. They showed a variety of expressions and movements, which Rosa carefully sketched. The terrified noises the cattle made disturbed the sensitive artist.

Because women were restricted by law, Rosa had to obtain a police permit so she could wear trousers while she drew in the slaughterhouses. She also chose to wear her hair cropped short. And she rode her horse astride, rather than sidesaddle.

Rosa Bonheur. **Cow.**
No date. Pencil on paper.
7¾ × 9⅞ inches.
The Chrysler Museum,
Norfolk, Virginia.

18

But Rosa's style didn't interfere with her success. One of her canvases was awarded third prize in the Salon of 1845. Suddenly her paintings began to bring high prices.

Three years later Rosa indeed became a famous artist. Her painting *Cows and Bulls of the Cantal* received the gold medal in the Salon of 1848. It was the beginning of prosperity and good fortune for Rosa Bonheur. Shortly afterward, she received a three-thousand-franc commission from the state for a painting on the subject of plowing. *Plowing in the Nivernais* became one of Rosa's most famous paintings. Never again would Raymond worry about his daughter's ability to earn a living as an artist.

Auguste Bonheur. **Raymond Bonheur at Fifty-three.** *1849. Oil. Anna Klumpke. Photograph: Princeton University Libraries. Marquand Library.* Rosa's brother painted this portrait of their father the same year that Raymond died.

In 1849 Raymond died of heart disease. Rosa was glad that her father had lived to see his dream come true — his daughter's artwork had become even more popular than that of Elisabeth Vigée-Lebrun.

In fact, Raymond's efforts to encourage women artists had grown beyond his family. When her father died, Rosa took over his directorship of the School of Drawing for Young Girls. She and Juliette taught for the next ten years in this free school funded by the city of Paris.

Soon after Raymond's death, Rosa began an eighteen-month study of horses for her most spectacular painting, *The Horse Fair.* In a peasant smock and her trousers, she visited the horse markets outside Paris. She also studied at the Paris Omnibus Company, where she practiced drawing the workhorses that pulled the buses through the city.

Rosa chose a large canvas for *The Horse Fair,* and she filled the space by painting images of the spirited horses almost life-size. The restless subjects seem to charge toward the foreground of the composition, then turn to disappear into the background. As the heavy, rich colors and curved shapes are repeated on the canvas, their patterns help show movement and rhythm. In this way, Rosa unified her composition. With a bit of imagination, art critics could smell the dust, feel the ground rumble, and hear the thundering of the horses' hooves.

The Horse Fair was the hit of the Salon of 1853, and two years later it sold for forty thousand francs. In fact, the painting became so popular that England's Queen Victoria asked to view it in London. So Rosa, with her lifetime friend Nathalie, followed the artwork across the English Channel to visit the queen at Buckingham Palace.

Rosa Bonheur. **Study for
"The Horse Fair."** *No date.
Black chalk, gray wash,
heightened with white, on beige
paper. 5⅜ × 13¼
inches. The Metropolitan
Museum of Art, bequest of
Edith H. Proskauer, 1975
(1975.319.2).*

Rosa Bonheur. **The Horse
Fair.** *1853. Oil 96¼ ×
199½ inches. The
Metropolitan Museum of
Art, New York, gift of
Cornelius Vanderbilt, 1887.
This large canvas caught
the attention of all who
attended the Salon of 1853.*

When Rosa saw that the queen and others in England and Scotland loved her painting, she returned to France even more determined to create other works of art. Now that Rosa had achieved fame and fortune as an artist, she and Nathalie purchased a château (sha-TOE). In this charming French country house, they lived the rest of their lives.

The grounds of the large château were bordered by forest, and Rosa walked every day along a shady lane. She sketched almost every rock and tree in the forest. She painted images of the deer and wild boar at sunset and sometimes hunted wild game with her rifle.

Château de By, near Fontainebleau. *Anna Klumpke. Photograph: Princeton University Libraries. Marquand Library.* In 1860, from her earnings as an artist, Rosa joined Nathalie in purchasing this spacious French château built in the fifteenth century. Rosa loved the château and the many animals that she kept on its grounds. She would live the rest of her life in the Château de By.

Inside the grounds Rosa kept a menagerie of dogs, Icelandic ponies, wild mustang ponies, deer, elk, horses, sheep, gazelles, bulls, cows, monkeys, a yak, a boar, an eagle, and a lion. During these happy years at the château, she created paintings of all of her animals. The lion was her favorite subject.

Rosa Bonheur. **The King of the Desert.** *No date. Oil on canvas. 39³⁄₈ × 37⁵⁄₈ inches. The FORBES Magazine Collection, New York.*

Rosa liked to portray her animal subjects in many moods. For this pose, Rosa had to observe one of her lions as it roared and memorize its facial expression so she could paint it later.

As a grown woman, Rosa was five feet tall with brown hair and dark eyes. She had a high forehead, a large nose, and a firm jawline. In 1857 artist Edouard-Louis Dubufe knew that Rosa Bonheur's fame as an artist would be long lasting. He asked Rosa to pose for a portrait, and she kindly agreed.

When Rosa saw the finished portrait, in which her arm rested on a table, she thought the painting was boring. Dubufe agreed to let her experiment with his canvas. To shift the emphasis in Dubufe's painting, Rosa — with her tongue-in-cheek sense of humor — brushed out the image of the table and painted in an image of her favorite bull. Dubufe entered the portrait in the Salon of 1857, where an art collector paid eight thousand francs to Dubufe for the portrait and seven thousand francs to Rosa for her addition of the image of the bull.

Rosa had become well known for her strong will, artistic talent, and sense of humor. She was admired in her village and in all of France. In 1865 Rosa Bonheur became the first woman ever to receive the medal of the French Legion of Honor. Emperor Louis-Napoléon had refused to award a woman this white enamel five-pointed star attached to a red ribbon, which symbolized membership in the honor society of the French Republic. However, he allowed Empress Eugénie to present the medal to Rosa in his absence.

Edouard-Louis Dubufe.
Portrait of Rosa Bonheur.
1857. Oil on canvas. Musée du Château de Versailles.
© Photo R.M.N.
Rosa asked the artist Dubufe if she could experiment with his portrait of her. She brushed out the image of a table and painted in the image of her favorite bull.

Rosa Bonheur. **Sheep by the Sea.** *1869. Oil on cradled panel. 12¾ × 18 inches. The National Museum of Women in the Arts. Gift of Wallace and Wilhelmina Holladay.*
In this painting we see Rosa's realistic style of portraying animals. The sheep appear calm and relaxed in their natural surroundings.

Although Rosa enjoyed public admiration, she insisted upon keeping her privacy as an artist. Sometimes she liked to visit the seashore alone to create calm and restful scenes. In her oil painting *Sheep by the Sea,* the relaxed subjects are settled in a meadow by the water. It is easy to imagine where the light comes from simply by looking at the sheep. The soft texture of the wool is highlighted with light color values. By adding dark color values below, Rosa created contrast to show the round and full forms of the sheep. And she created dark shadows against the glistening grass.

Rosa painted parts of the land and animals in the foreground with yellow and orange, the warm colors of her palette. To paint the sea in the middle ground and the sky in the background, she used cool colors such as blue and violet.

Rosa liked to combine her paintings of landscapes with scenes of farm and peasant life. In *Gathering for the Hunt*, she created a feeling of energy and movement among her subjects. The hunters, horses, and dogs signal to each other that they are ready and eager to romp across the fields. Even though the sun itself is not seen in the painting, the viewer can imagine a hidden light source, which brightens the sky.

Rosa Bonheur. **Gathering for the Hunt.** *1856. Oil on canvas. 30½ × 58⅛ inches. Haggin Collection. The Haggin Museum. Stockton, California.*
In this early-morning painting, Rosa merely suggests a light source. The rising sun can be imagined by the viewer through the highlights and shadows on the canvas.

Artist unknown. **Napoléon, Bonheur, and Buffalo Bill.** *1898. Lithograph. 26½ × 39¼ inches. Courier Lithographic Company. Buffalo, New York. Courtesy of the Library of Congress, Washington, D.C.* This playbill illustration of Buffalo Bill's Wild West Show in Paris purposely portrays Rosa in a setting that was not possible in real life. She sits between the emperor Napoléon, who had died in defeat many years before, and the dashing Buffalo Bill Cody, who now captured the attention of Parisians.

During Rosa's later years, an exciting event came her way. In 1889 Colonel Buffalo Bill Cody traveled from America to Paris to perform his Wild West Show. His company for the show included 115 Native Americans, 48 cowboys, of whom 16 were musicians, 6 women who could ride or shoot, half a dozen vaqueros (Mexican cowboys), and other hired hands. He also traveled with 20 buffalo, 25 mustangs, 8 dogs, and 186 horses.

For the entire seven-month run of the show, Rosa visited Buffalo Bill's camp on a thirty-five-acre field near Paris. With Buffalo Bill's permission, she sketched images of the horses and bison and Native Americans. Before he left Paris, Buffalo Bill visited Rosa at her château, where he posed for a portrait. This painting of Buffalo Bill Cody was shown on playbills, postcards, and posters.

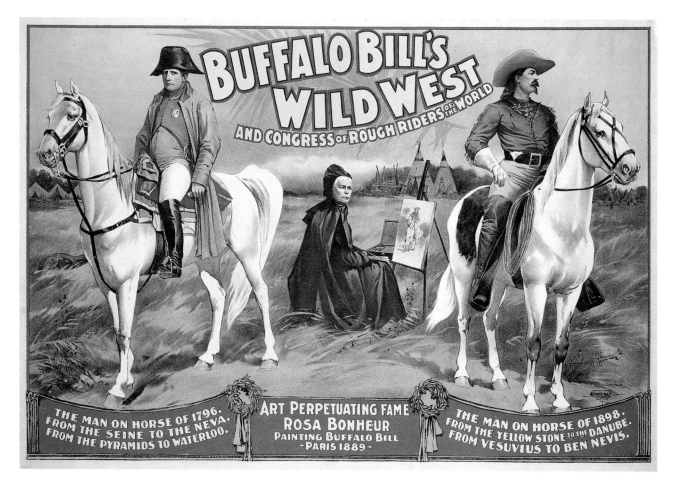

Rosa Bonheur. **Colonel William F. Cody.** 1889. *Oil on canvas.* *18½ × 15¼ inches.* *Buffalo Bill Historical Center, Cody, Wyoming.* When Rosa completed this portrait of Buffalo Bill on his favorite horse, he immediately sent the painting to his wife in Nebraska. The story goes that when he later learned that his home was on fire, he wired this message: "Save the Rosa Bonheur and let the flames take the rest."

Rosa Bonheur. **The Duel.**
*1895. Oil on canvas. 59 ×
96 inches. The Warner
Collection of Gulf States Paper
Corporation, Tuscaloosa,
Alabama.*
Toward the end of her life,
Rosa continued to paint
images of horses. She
especially enjoyed showing
the spirited animals in
action.

For the rest of her own happy life, Rosa used the
studies she had made during her seven months with
Buffalo Bill's company. In her studio at the château,
she accepted commissions from art collectors in
America, who asked that she paint scenes from the
Wild West. When she was seventy-three, Rosa asked
her artist-friend, Anna Klumpke, who traveled to
America, to bring back some wild sagebrush so that
Rosa could finish her painting of wild horses fleeing a
prairie fire.

In 1899 Rosa became ill with pneumonia. Within
several days, she died at her château. The world was
saddened to lose this legendary woman, but Rosa
Bonheur's reputation as a famous artist would
continue to inspire others a century later.

When the 1,835 paintings in her studio were auctioned, there were 255 studies of horses, 94 of dogs, 238 of cows and bulls, 221 of wild beasts, 221 of deer, 250 landscapes with animals, and many studies of Native Americans. These works of art earned high praise during Rosa's lifetime because they reflected her belief that nature is always true and beautiful.

Rosa Bonheur. **Royalty at Home.** *1885. Watercolor. 15½ × 22 inches. The Minneapolis Institute of Arts.* In Rosa's estate sale, paintings and drawings of lions and many other animals were auctioned. This painting shows Rosa's lions in a peaceful mood.

This headline appeared in the *New York Herald* Paris edition of May 31, 1890. The two-column story reported that the gallery was filled with buyers from many countries.

Anna Elizabeth Klumpke
(1856–1942). **Rosa
Bonheur.** *1898. Oil on
canvas. 46⅛ × 38⅝
inches. The Metropolitan
Museum of Art. Gift of the
artist in memory of Rosa
Bonheur, 1922.*

During the last year of her life, at the age of
seventy-six, Rosa agreed to let her friend Anna
Klumpke paint her portrait. In the portrait, Rosa
wears her Legion of Honor medal, as well as the
rosette she received as her second Legion of Honor
award. Rosa posed for the portrait beside her last
canvas, *La Foulaison,* which she was not able to
finish. The canvas hangs today in her studio at the
Château de By.